AF272984

the
Hat
Book

the Hat Book

 PAPADAKIS

First published in Great Britain in 2011 by Papadakis Publisher
An imprint of New Architecture Group Limited

Kimber Studio, Winterbourne, Berkshire, RG20 8AN, UK

Tel. +44 (0) 1635 248833

info@papadakis.net
www.papadakis.net

Publishing Director: Alexandra Papadakis
Design Director: Aldo Sampieri
Editor: Sheila de Vallée
Editorial and Research: Caroline Kuhtz
Research Assistant: Juliana Kassianos
Production Assistant: Stefano Rosignoli

ISBN 978 1 906506 20 9

Copyright © Papadakis Publisher
Text © Stephanie Talbot
All rights reserved.

No part of this publication may be reproduced or transmitted in any form or
by any means, electronic or mechanical, including photocopy, recording or
any other information storage and retrieval system, without prior permission
in writing from the Publisher.

Printed and bound in China

Contents

Introduction

It is impossible to imagine Queen Elizabeth II without a colourful hat with upturned brim, Jackie Kennedy *sans* her trademark pillbox, Al Capone without a fedora, John Wayne without a Stetson, Tiger Woods without a Swoosh-adorned baseball cap, Pierrot without his skull cap, Charlie Chaplin – or Snoopy for that matter – without a British bowler balanced confidently on his head.

The spectrum of shapes and silhouettes that comprises what is honoured with the title 'hat' is vast and also, to some extent, gendered. Both men and women may have worn flamboyant plumes on their heads during Tudor times, but fast forward to the twenty-first century and feathers in millinery are reserved for fancy dress and/or the flamboyant.

One of the first pictorial recordings of a hat appears in an Egyptian tomb painting at Thebes showing a man wearing a coolie-style straw hat. Hats also featured in the art of other ancient civilisations including China, Greece and Rome. Centuries later head coverings became synonymous with battle, shielding warriors from injury. The trajectory of the hat

since then is both rich and fascinating, illustrating social mores and shifts in sartorial trends, which in themselves reflect changes in social behaviour and conventions.

Hats are an iconic feature of the visual landscape we encounter in day-to-day life, principally because their very presence creates an identity for the wearer. Throughout history, hats in their many incarnations as well as their affiliations with different cultures, have characterised social standing, authorial status, rank in society, and they have been worn as ceremonial attire. However, their use straddles not only symbolic representation and mandatory protection from climate conditions but is imbued with an aesthetic value that continues to captivate.

A Brief History of Hats

Throughout history hats have been the subject of many a poem, song, quote and storyline; Dr Seuss's *Cat in the Hat* would not have quite the same resonance if the said cat had not worn a hat!

Now, although a range of headgear, including veils, kerchiefs, caps, wimples and hoods had been a common sight for centuries, it was only after 1300 that both men and women adopted the hat for general outdoor use. For men hats became a fashion item for the first time and the more wealthy citizens in the towns were to be seen in elaborate hats that had evolved from the hoods of previous centuries.

Women still wore the wimple that had been brought to Europe from the Middle East by the Crusaders but it had been transformed into the decorative headdresses we associate with the Middle Ages by the addition of padded rolls and tall forms built on frames often constructed into elaborate shapes such as cones, horns and hearts, with veiling draped over the top. However resplendent, one can only suspect the effect of such a burden on the wearer's spine! Cauls (a type of hairnet made of fabric or netted cord) were also popular. Thankfully, by 1500 hats had returned to a more simple design, or at least simpler in comparison with the spectacles of the previous century.

The most fashionable hats for men in the sixteenth century were made made of soft fabric and had a gathered crown and were often decorated with a feather or a jewel. They became taller as the century progressed and as the hat came to reflect the wearer's rank in society. Women continued to wear hats and veils but also sported coifs (a close-fitting embroidered or lace-trimmed linen cap tied under the chin), which were worn under other hats or hoods. Some women's hats at this time borrowed their style from masculine fashion.

In the seventeenth century at the royal court and in other fashionable circles men's hats had flatter crowns and wider brims. They were made of felt and embellished with long, drooping ostrich feathers or ribbons. These were eventually supplanted by the tricorne, a three-cornered hat which remained popular, probably because of its practicality, until the next century among both the civilian and military populations. It was replaced by the bicorne.

The latter part of the seventeenth century, especially in France under King Louis XIV, saw the emergence of elaborate, powdered wigs as both a fashion and power statement and hats were relegated to the role of a mere accessory carried under a gentleman's arm so as not to disrupt his coiffure, or perched daintily on a woman's vertiginous, highly-decorated hairpiece. There is a legend that in 1776 the roof of the main entrance to St. Paul's Cathedral had to be raised four feet in order to accommodate the extravagance of high society's hairstyles.

The eighteenth century also saw a variety of more modest headgear that did not require a lady-in-waiting to supervise any potential dangers of hair catching fire. For those not born into the aristocracy, wide-brimmed straw hats tied with a ribbon under the chin as well as bonnets made of pleated taffeta or silk and structured upon hoops of cane or whalebone were commonplace.

From 1780 onwards, simple cotton bonnets became fashionable at all levels of society, especially in France, following the French Revolution (1789) where ostentatious hairstyles and hats were associated unfavourably with the aristocracy. Bonnets resisted the vagaries of fashion for over a century; they were fashioned out of velvet, lace and straw and embellished with ribbons, flowers, feathers and gauze trims. The status of the wearer was implied through the tasteful coordination of bonnet and dress.

As the nineteenth century approached structured hats such as the top hat and bowler were worn by middle and upper class gentlemen in England, whilst women sported straw boaters and trilbies, previously considered men's hats. The fashion for feathers in women's hats was also widespread, especially as plumes had now become a status symbol.

During the Edwardian era (1901-1910) a return to large and lavish hats saw favour, with tulle, ribbons and flowers used en masse. Etiquette and formality played a big part in the wearing of hats on a daily basis. Women, especially, often changed their hats several times a day. Regardless of age or financial background hats were worn by all; only beggars went bareheaded and even then used a cap to collect spare change. And as for the concept of *hatiquette*, in the early 1600s it was acceptable to wear hats indoors, but after 1680 the hat was kept solely for outdoor wear.

By the 1920s women's hats were generally plain, as ostentatious decoration was frowned upon and seen as unpatriotic. Cloche hats were particularly fashionable. Often made from felt or straw, they were very closely fitted and worn low down on the head, which complemented the fashion for shorter haircuts and flatter styles. Increased trade between

Upon an ambler
easily she sat,
Y-wimpled well,
and on her head an hat
As broad as is a
buckler or a targe.

Geoffrey Chaucer
The Wife of Bath

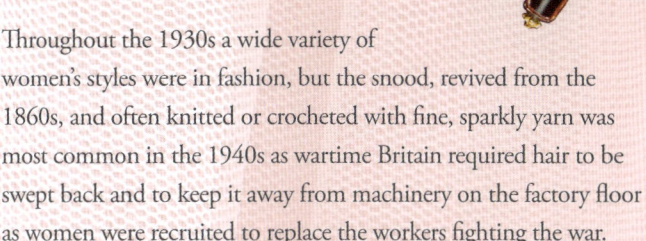

Britain and India in the 1790s had introduced the turban to English fashion and its popularity increased once again.

Throughout the 1930s a wide variety of women's styles were in fashion, but the snood, revived from the 1860s, and often knitted or crocheted with fine, sparkly yarn was most common in the 1940s as wartime Britain required hair to be swept back and to keep it away from machinery on the factory floor as women were recruited to replace the workers fighting the war.

However, feathers, veiling and artificial flowers were also popular, even though by the 1940s hats were generally no longer practical as people had to rush to air raid shelters. Social conventions were set aside and though hat materials were no longer rationed, the wearing of hats decreased after the war.

During the 1950s wide brimmed sunhats were often worn, as well as small hats fitted close to the head.

In the early 1960s, pillbox hats and puffs of veil with bows or small flowers accented the large beehive and bouffant hairstyles that were in vogue. Towards the end of the decade, slouchy Bakerboy caps and sunhats with floppy brims were the must-have item; however, by the 1970s hats had largely been abandoned in favour of loose, flowing locks.

The last three decades have seen the hat's popularity fluctuate but with the current climate endorsing individuality every imagin-able style is acceptable in the name of fashion.

LOCK & CO
Hats

**EXCLUSIVE STYLES
FOR LADIES & GENTLEMEN**

Catalogue available
(Please quote C2)

**Visit us at Stand 115
Goodwood Revival**

6 ST. JAMES'S STREET LONDON SWIA 1EF
0207 930 8874
www.lockhatters.co.uk

Advertisement produced from an original 1950's showcard

24

LOCK & CO
Hats

EXCLUSIVE STYLES
FOR LADIES &
GENTLEMEN

6 ST. JAMES'S STREET LONDON SW1A 1EF
0207 930 8874
www.lockhatters.co.uk

Advertisement produced from an original 1950's showcard

25

Now—Ten thousand, and ten thousand times ten thousand (for matter and motion are infinite) are the ways by which a hat may be dropped upon the ground, without any effect.—Had he flung it, or thrown it, or cast it, or skimmed it, or squirted it, or let it slip or fall in any possible direction under heaven,—or in the best direction that could be given to it,—had he dropped it like a goose—like a puppy—like an ass—or in doing it, or even after he had done, had he looked like a fool—like a ninny—like a nincompoop—it had fail'd, and the effect upon the heart had been lost.

Lawrence Sterne, Tristram Shandy

Look here, I have bought this bonnet. I do not think it is very pretty; but I thought I might as well buy it as not. I shall pull it to pieces as soon as I get home, and see if I can make it up any better.

Jane Austen, Pride & Prejudice

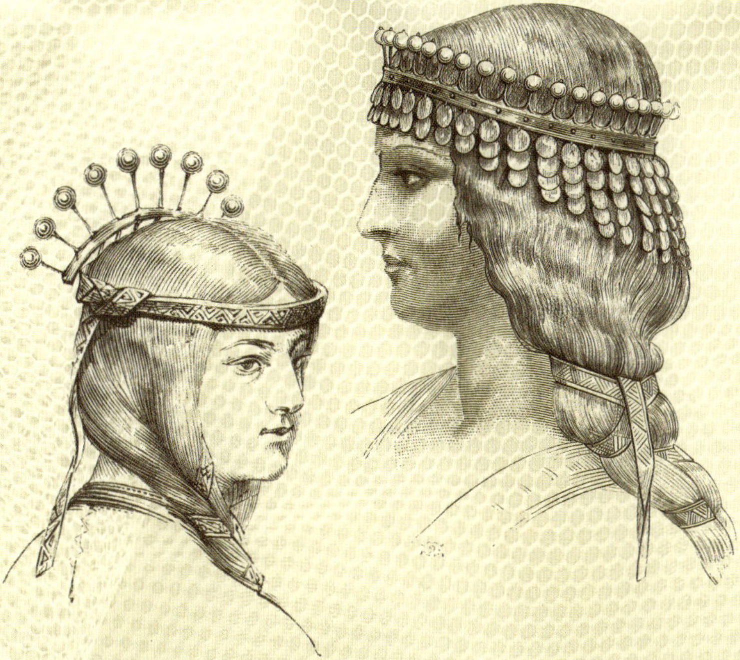

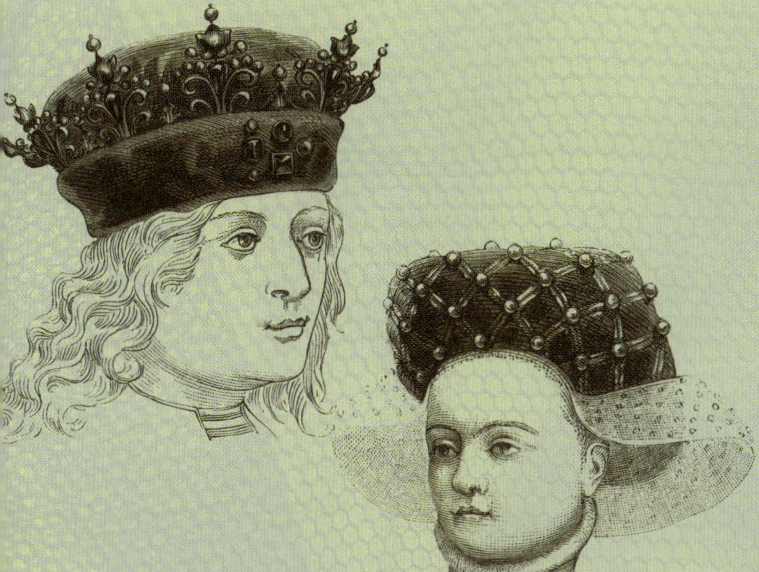

Why, she invents hats for me. You remember the one I wore at Lady Hilstone's garden-party? You don't, but it's nice of you to pretend that you do. Well, she made it out of nothing. All good hats are made out of nothing.

Oscar Wilde, The Picture of Dorian Gray

On the top of the Crumpetty Tree
The Quangle Wangle sat,
But his face you could not see
On account of his Beaver Hat.

For his Hat was a hundred and two feet wide,
With ribbons and bibbons on every side,
And bells, and buttons, and loops, and lace,
So that nobody ever could see the face
Of the Quangle Wangle Quee.

Edward Lear

Iconic Hats

One point of view from which to consider the importance of the
hat is to trace historical episodes through the presence of iconic
hats, since hats point both to sartorial trends and also social
behaviour and cultural shifts.

Author Lewis Carroll's classic *Alice in Wonderland* (1865) saw
its 'Mad Tea-Party' scene feature a Hatter wearing an informal
version of the most popular hat of the day: the top hat. Although
known as 'the Mad Hatter', Carroll had not conceived that name
for this boisterous character referring to him only as 'the hatter'.
However, the phrase 'mad as a hatter' was common in Carroll's
time; its origin probably alludes to the fact that hatters often did
go senile because they had been poisoned by the mercury that
was frequently used in the making of hats.

Another familiar fictitious character is author Sir Arthur Conan
Doyle's Sherlock Holmes (1887). Resplendent in his deerstalker,
this London-based detective is so synonymous with this type of hat,
typically worn in rural areas, that the hat itself has equally become
synonymous with a stereotypical hat of a detective! Conan Doyle's
stories do not actually describe Holmes wearing a deerstalker
per se, but without the imagery of Holmes in his flexible, ear-
flapped cap, one has to ask whether Sherlock Holmes would be so
illustrious. In recent years pop musician and costume enthusiast

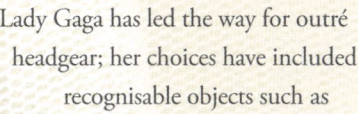

Lady Gaga has led the way for outré headgear; her choices have included recognisable objects such as giant antelope horns assembled out of feathers, a telephone fashioned from polygonal leather, an orbital construction, a metallic lightning shape a couple of feet high and a diamanté-encrusted lobster. Gaga's penchant for the theatrical borrows from the Surrealist movement, the cultural movement of the early twentieth century that juxtaposed unexpected elements to provoke political and social thought. Famously, artist Salvador Dalí designed an upturned-shoe hat for Italian fashion designer Elsa Schiaparelli (circa 1937) which stunned the then-conservative world of fashion and has since been cited as a radical fashion piece. However, it is worth noting that during the late eighteenth century reign of Louis XVI, Marie Antoinette favoured decadent head creations including a ship embellished with feathers to salute the French Navy's Tall Ships. And in the first decade of the twentieth century in England whole stuffed birds were sometimes used as decoration for the most fashionable hats.

Fast forward to 2011 and once again it is a member of royalty who has divided a nation's opinion on the subject of sartorial taste based on the wearing of a hat. Princess Beatrice's silk Philip Treacy creation worn at her cousin Prince William's wedding to Kate Middleton caused such a furore that numerous Facebook pages have been devoted to it. Princess Beatrice turned the tables by putting the offending hat up for sale on ebay and donating the proceeds (£80,000) to her favourite charity.

Cœffure
à l'Independance ou le
Triomphe de la liberté

Oh, what a hat!

Edward Lear, Book of Nonsense

I would

never give up

my wigs and hats

for anything

Lady Gaga

Wherever I lay my hat that's my home

Marvin Gaye

Haute Couture

The legendary Coco Chanel began her career as a milliner. It is somewhat ironic that such a revolutionary whose clientele belonged to the upper echelons of Paris society, herself was born into a modest background.

As a young woman Coco Chanel launched her millinery business by making hats for her friends to wear at social occasions. In 1910, aged 23, she began selling hats from her own shop in Paris. Her most popular creation was a little boater that she adorned as simply as possible; an antithesis to the ornate fashions that were heralded at the time. Chanel's aesthetic introduced a more casual and practical attitude to fashion without compromising the essence of what it meant to be stylish. She has been credited with being the first designer to establish black as a fashion colour. Within ten years her business had expanded to include a couture house, her own textile factory and a line of perfumes that included the famous Chanel No. 5.

In the years since Chanel's renowned breakthrough, hats have continued to be a mainstay in fashion and have continued to be subject to social and sartorial trends.

The term 'milliner', someone who makes hats, is derived from the city of Milan in Italy, where the best hats were traditionally made in the eighteenth century. A milliner would not only create

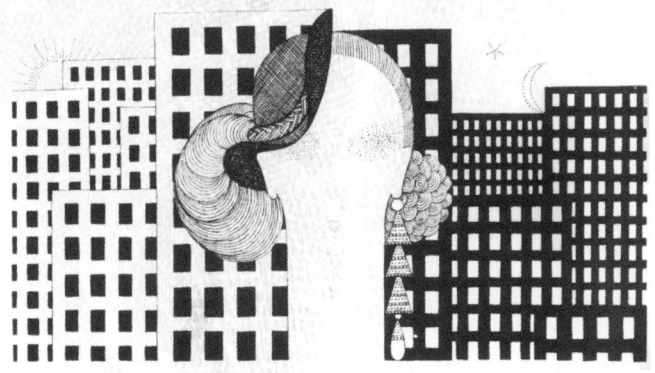

hats and bonnets, but select lace, trimmings and other accessories to complement an outfit. Technically, a hatmaker makes hats for men, and a milliner makes hats for women and traditionally, millinery was a woman's occupation… however, in recent years at least three British milliners have become household names the world over, having revived the popularity of exquisite hats for special occasions. Whether or not you are a hat-wearing enthusiast the names of David Shilling, Stephen Jones and Phillip Treacy are likely to be familiar:

David Shilling's hats are always present on Ladies' Day at Royal Ascot. Jones's sophisticated and theatrical designs bring the playful into the world of millinery through his engagement with scale, fabric choices and the use of themes. He has collaborated with Vivienne Westwood, Thierry Mugler, Jean-Paul Gaultier and John Galliano for Dior and was commissioned to make the critically acclaimed headpieces for musician Kylie Minogue's 2006 Showgirl tour.

Treacy's hats are sculptural and visionary and have featured on the most prestigious fashion catwalks including Chanel, Valentino, Alexander McQueen and Givenchy as well as the heads of royalty and Hollywood stars. Treacy's muse, the late fashion doyenne Isabella Blow, is reported to have been buried in one of Treacy's creations.

It's not a mad hatter's tea party. It's meant to be a sensual, erotic display. You're there to get a new husband, a new boyfriend, a new girlfriend, whatever. And you can get it. The hat is a means to an end, a marriage contract. It's everything. It's a sensual thing — the idea of catching somebody like a spider in a web. It's the old fashioned cock-and-hen story, the mating dance. Men love hats.

Isabella Blow

Cock your hat -
angles are attitudes

Frank Sinatra

1918
1930

LES VOLUTES
LES VOLUPTÉS
DE L'ART DÉCO

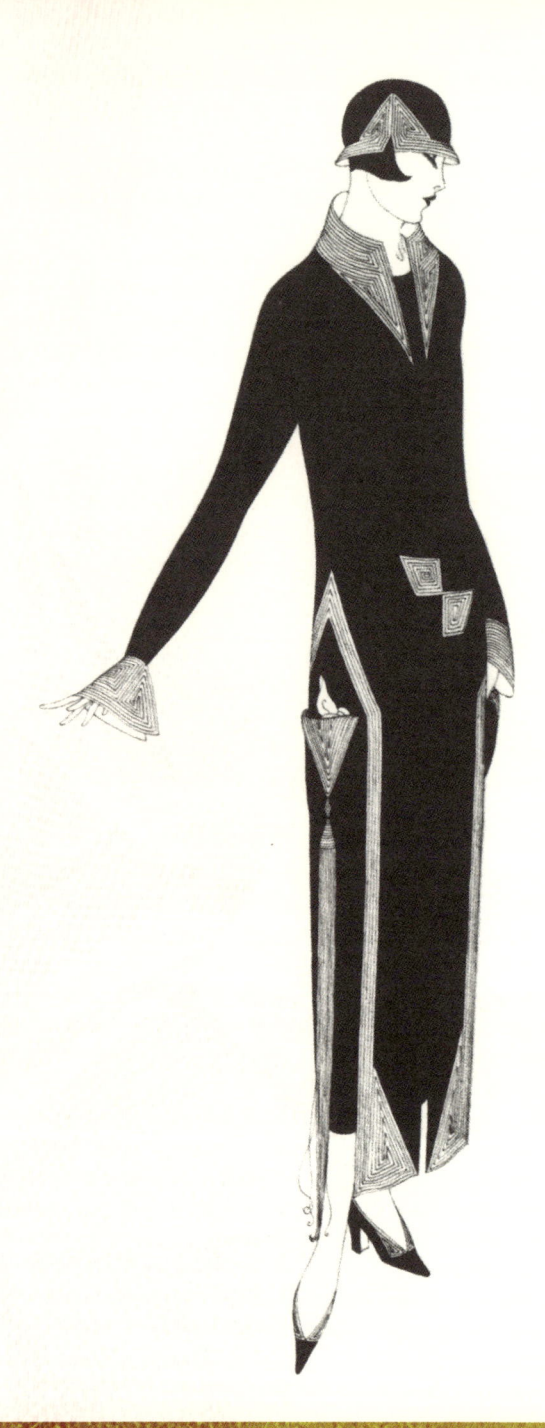

If a woman

rebels against high heeled

shoes, she should

take care to do it in

a very smart hat

George Bernard Shaw

A cheaper and
less painful form of
plastic surgery

Isabella Blow

Everyone has

a head so everyone

has a possibility to

wear a hat and you

feel good in a hat

Philip Treacy

101

Créations
Charlotte
Cruchot
265 rue St Honoré - Paris -

In Wyoming it is illegal to wear
a hat in public theaters or places
of amusement that obstructs
another persons' view.

I myself

have 12 hats,

and each

one represents a

different personality

Margaret Atwood

LES
CLAIRS
CHAPEAUX
D'ÉTÉ

The hat is
the ultimum
moriens of
respectability

Oliver Wendell Holmes

Saying you don't look good in a hat is like saying you don't look good in shoes!

Anonymous

A number of
ladies in summer
dresses and
gentlemen in grey
frock-coats and tall
hats stood on the
lawn or sat upon
the benches

Edith Wharton,
The Age of Innocence

It
is impossible for
a hatless woman
to be chic
Emily Post

I have a hat. It is graceful
and feminine and gives me a
certain dignity, as if I were
attending a state funeral or
something. Someday I may
get up enough courage to wear it,
instead of carrying it

Erma Bombeck

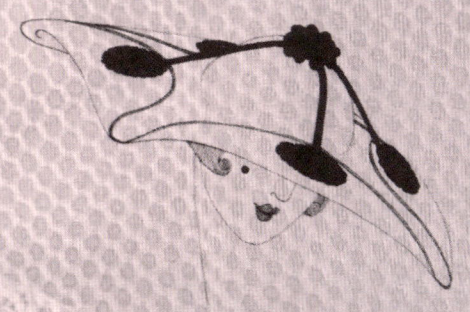

Hats

were associated

with old ladies and

I thought that was

crazy

Philip Treacy

I t's not the shape of

the woman's face that

really decides, but the

attitude of the hat

Frank Olive

Wearing hats has

become like fine art for me

Tina Brown

Hats are all about novelty, it's what makes the world turn around

Stephen Jones

Wearing a hat versus
not wearing a hat is the
difference between looking
adequate and looking
your best

Martha Sliter

All the hats now were
immense; covered with
fruits and flowers and
all manner of birds.

Marcel Proust, Swann's Way

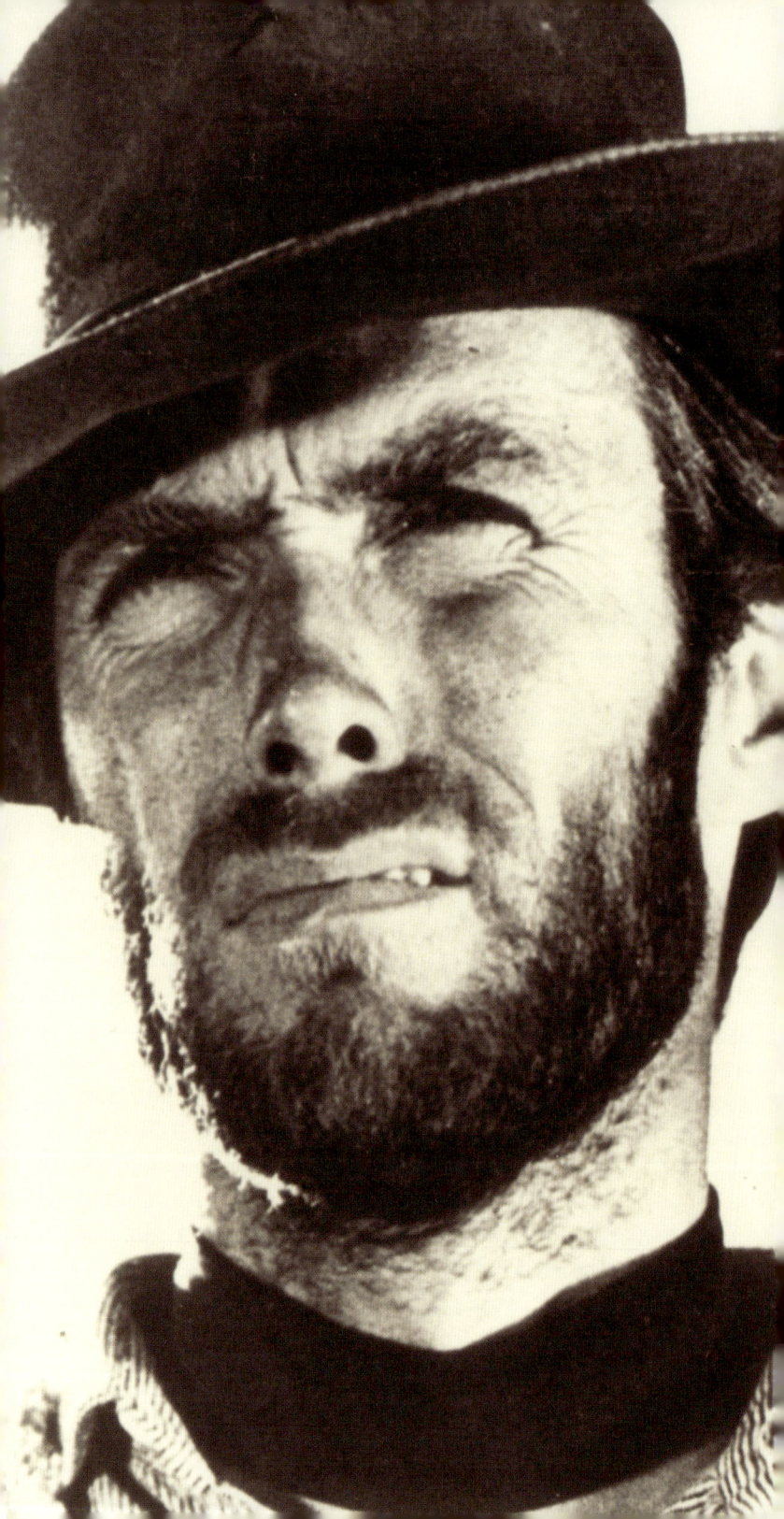

Hats in Cinema

Hats are not only superb items to complete a 'look' or outfit, they are great props to dance with to express a gesture with or to animate an emotion. In 1814, Louis Comte, a French magician, became the first person to pull a white rabbit out of a top hat and where would a cracker be without the mandatory paper hat…

At the beginning of the nineteenth century, in England, the top hat symbolised wealth and status, its height and minimalist appearance giving a certain gravitas to the wearer. A century later the top hat reappeared as an emblem of the debonair male Hollywood stars performing extravagant routines with top hats that appeared glued to their scalps as they moved across the cinema screens. However, the top hat transgressed its relationship as a male item of apparel when movie star Marlene Dietrich wore one partnered with a male dinner suit in the 1930 film *Morocco*. Despite the top hat disappearing as an everyday form of apparel, it is still worn to mark special occasions.

The Panama, Trilby, Fedora, Stetson, and to some extent Sombrero, although vastly different in their cultural heritage and social overtones all seem to belong to a similar language of hats. All sport a quasi-triangulated crown and broad brim and essentially their form has been unchanged since their inception.

Although originating from Mexico and made to protect workers from the sun, the Sombrero straw hat (the name is derived

from 'sombra', the Spanish word for shade), was 'westernised' when actors such as Clint Eastwood wore them in blockbuster films. Famously worn by Mariachi musicians the Sombrero became the stereotypical Mexican hat and is credited as the inspiration for the quintessential cowboy hat: the Stetson.

The Stetson is credited to John B. Stetson who in 1866 created the legendary, open-crowned, flat-brimmed model forever associated with Texas and the Wild West protagonists of Buffalo Bill, Annie Oakley and Calamity Jane.

Other hats linked with a particular type of culture are the Fedora and its narrower brimmed counterpart, the Trilby. Gangster culture adopted these styles of hats as their sartorial leitmotif and in the last twenty years have been assimilated as markers of 'gangsta' culture by the likes of Mos Def. Justin Timberlake sports them as well as famed pop culture figures such as Johnny Depp and the late Michael Jackson who have been photographed wearing them. Likewise, jazz, ska as well as rude boy, mod and 2 Tone subcultures have all incorporated the Trilby into their visual imagery. Nowadays, both the Fedora and Trilby are worn by both men and women. Since women sported a version of them during the 1940s alongside men who wore the Panama as well, their retro connotation has propelled city streets to be witness to a large number of fashion-wise devotees.

Films are great vehicles in which hats can rise above their accessory value and actually become 'characters' in their own right. Art director Cecil Beaton's extravagant millinery for the 1964 film *My Fair Lady* is testimony to this. His visuals have become so iconic that it is unsurprising that he won an Academy Award (Oscar) for costume design. In June 2011 Audrey Hepburn's iconic black and white Ascot races dress, including matching hat, sold at auction for $3.7 million!

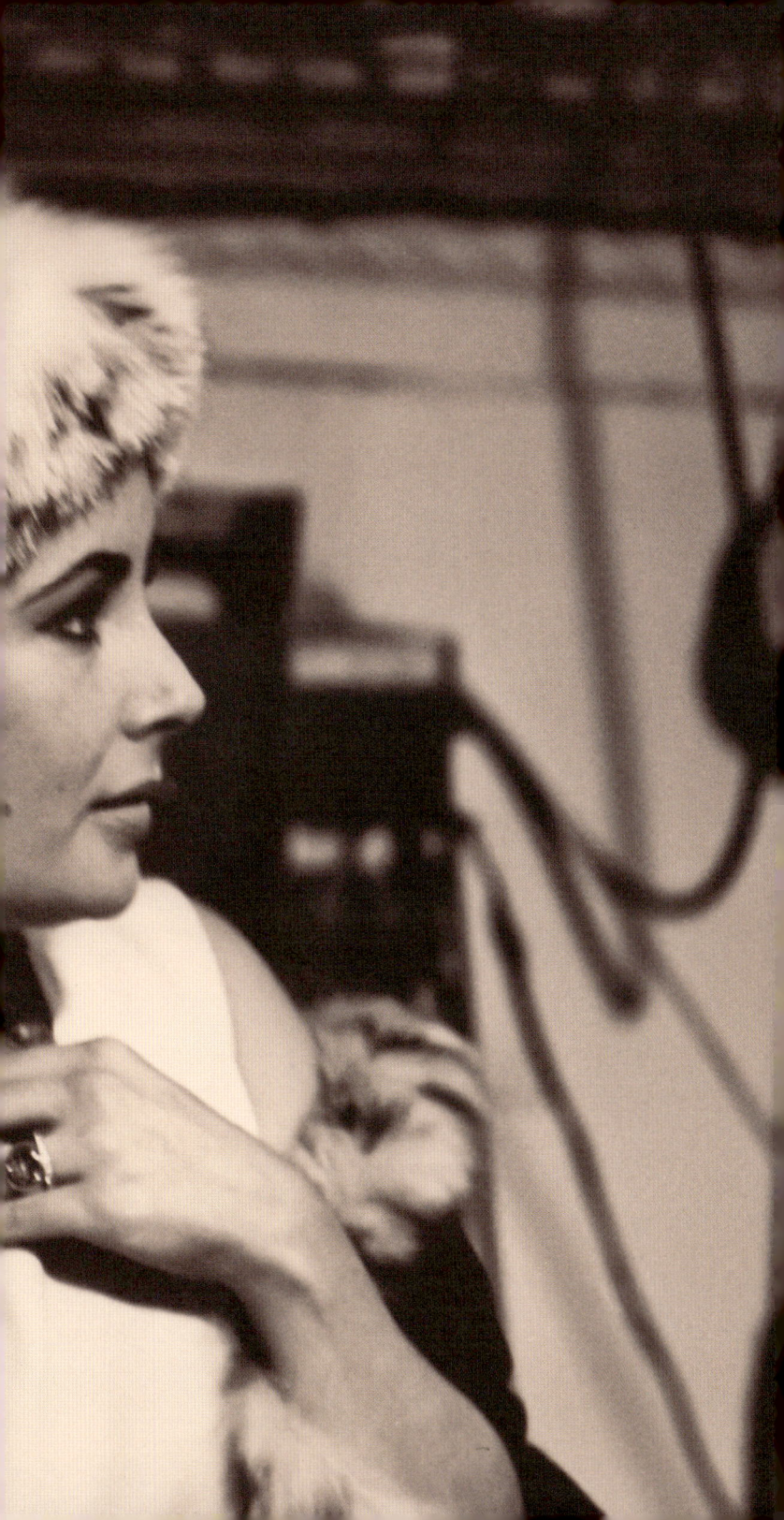

I'm

puttin' on
my Top Hat,
tyin' up my
white tie,
brushin' off
my tails

Fred Astaire
in Top Hat

Hats in Art

It is unsurprising that the visual fields of art and cinema have embraced a hat's ability to express a narrative or add colour to a frame. Many artists have painted themselves wearing a hat especially the members of the French nineteenth century art movement Impressionism and its early twentieth century successor the Post-Impressionists.

French culture has always favoured the hat as an accessory with which to finesse an outfit. The beret especially is associated with French Parisian as well as French rural life. Claude Monet's self-portraits often featured the beret fortifying its Francophile associations. The casual cap has also experienced fame through art, Paul Cézanne's iconic 1878-1880 painting of himself is entitled quite simply *Self Portrait in a White Cap*.

Generally made from wool, felt is one of the oldest known fabrics and started to be used when people discovered that fibres matted together when damp and warm could manifest as a robust

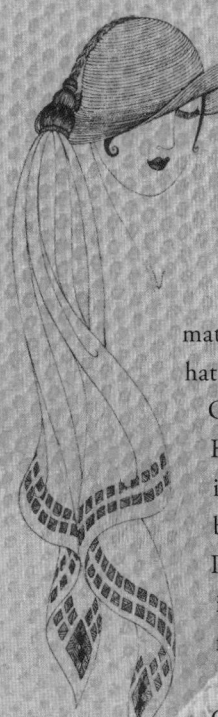

material, ideal for hoods and structured hats as popularised by artist Vincent van Gogh. In more recent years artist David Hockney is often seen sporting an insouciant straw hat embellished by a black band, and feted ceramicist Grayson Perry, whose propensity for cross-dressing is as well known as his art works, is quite frequently styled with a colourful bonnet.

Conversely, hats have transcended their status as apparel into being art works themselves. Philip Treacy's 2001 sculptural masterpiece, made from Venetian antique lace, is so dramatic and seductive that both its carefully staged photographic image and the hat itself revises the context of fashion being taken seriously as art.

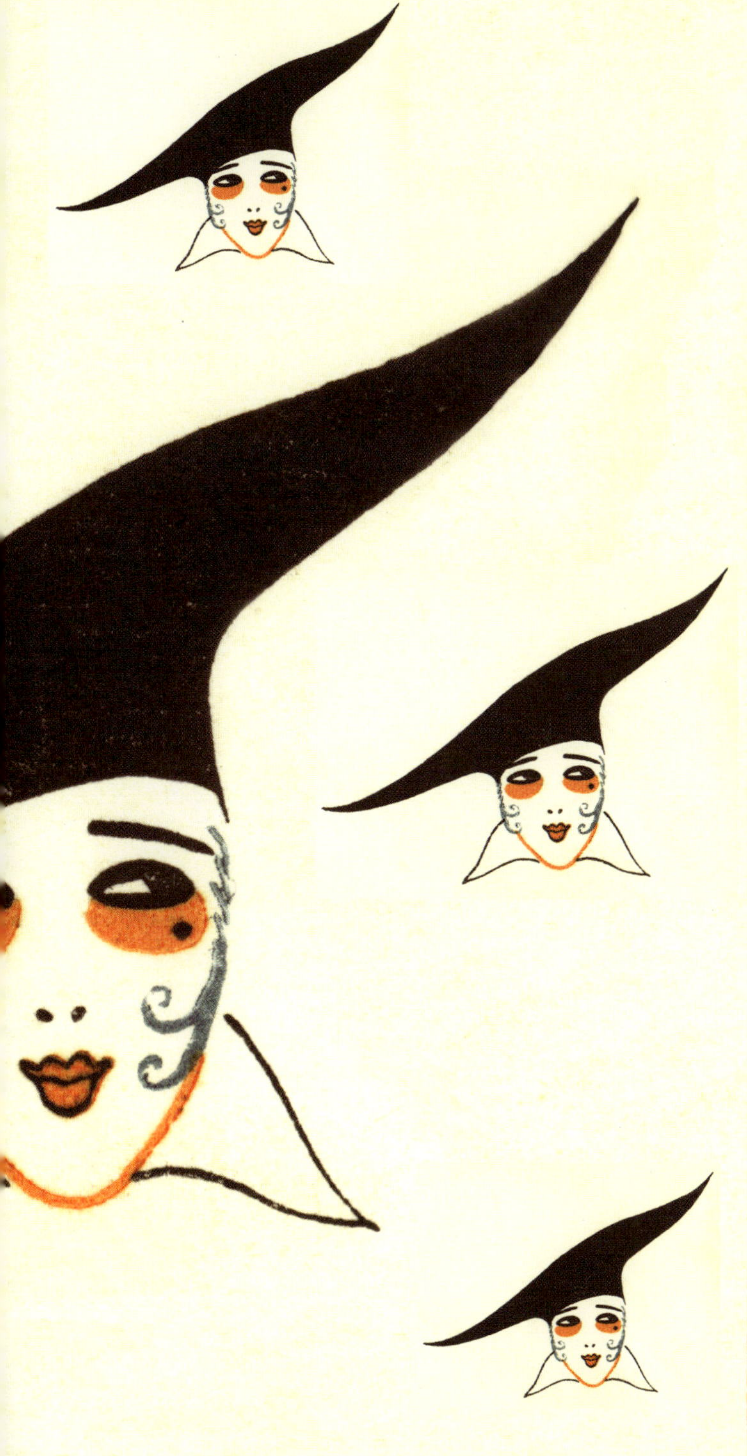

Y ou can flirt with a fan in your hand.
You can flirt holding a cigarette, too.
But a woman can really flirt with a hat.

Dolores Foster

DAVID

If

you're right,

I'll eat my hat!

Image Credits

Front cover, p172-173: Venetian antique lace wing hat © Philip Treacy 2001 couture show, Paris; endpapers, p22-23 (top & third row): from R. Broby-Johansen, *Body and Clothes: An Illustrated History of Costume*, Faber & Faber Ltd, 1968; pp1, 9 (left & right), 14, 16-17, 22-23 (second & forth row), 26 (top & bottom), 30, 31 (top & bottom), 32-33, 34-35, 38-39, 40-41, 44-45, 46, 48-49, 50-51, 52, 53, 54-55, 92 (all), 102-103, 104-105, 108-109, 112, 113, 114, 115, 116-117, 148, 162-163, 174-175, 176, 177, 186 (top): Collection Papadakis; pp2, 7, 37, 56, 58, 60, 62-63, 64-65, 72-73, 78, 152, 154, 156-157, 160, 164-165 © Getty Images; pp3, 6, 19, 20 (all), 27, 36, 42, 61, 120, 121: public domain; p4-5: Small Madonna hat in white straw © Philip Treacy 2001 couture show, Paris; pp8, 43, 90, 138-139, 192: from Jacques Sternberg and Pierre Chapelot, *Pin Up*, Academy and St Martin's Press, 1974 and Éditions Planète, 1971; p10: Flame of Desire Headpiece by Louis Mariette © photographed by Camille Sanson; pp11 (top), 15, 20 (bottom), 21 (top), 57, 79, 118 (top), 119 (bottom), 153, 167: © Penny Pins, www.pennypins. co.uk; pp11 (bottom), p13 (top & bottom), 168: from Jo Anne C. Day, *Decorative Silhouettes of the Twenties*, Dover Publications, 1975; p12: (top) Top Hat Panama Clown Pattern © Anthony Peto, photography by Olivier Brauman, (centre): Cracker Jack Felt Cow Print © Anthony Peto, photography by Olivier Brauman, (bottom): Wilcox African Wax Fabric © Anthony Peto, photography by Olivier Brauman; pp13 (middle), 21 (bottom), 81, 94, 110, 167 (bottom), 169 (all), 186 (bottom): from *Erte Fashions*, Academy Editions Ltd. and St. Martin's Press 1972; pp24, 25: © James Lock & Co, 6 St. James's Street, London SW1EF 0207 930 8874, www. lockhatters.co.uk; p28-29: Robert Gerlier (wearing the bowler hat) with his 'Classe Amicale', 1936; p59 (top and bottom): illustration by John Tenniel from *Alice's Adventures in Wonderland* by Lewis Carroll; p67: © AFP/Getty Images; p68-69: Tim Graham/Getty Images; p70-71: © courtesy of Paul Greenhalgh; p74-75: from Victor Arwas, *La Vie Parisienne*, Papadakis, 2010; pp77, 82: © WireImage; p80: Princess Neptune headpiece by Louis Mariette © photographed by Zena Holloway; p84-85: Titania headpiece by Louis Mariette © photographed by Philip Volkers; p86-87: Jade parisial cloche with matching feathers © Judy Bentinck, photographed by Alistair Cowin, www.alistaircowin.com; p88: Violetta © Gina Foster Millinery; p89: Amarige © Gina Foster Millinery; p91: Titania © Gina Foster Millinery; p93: Vervain hat worn by Erin O'Connor at the Investec Derby by Louis Mariette © photographed by Cameron McNee; p96-97: Pyramus headpiece by Louis Mariette © photographed by Philip Volkers; p98-99: Miss Tick Tock hat © Louis Mariette, photographed by Ross Perkins; p100: White feathered "hat" © Philip Treacy 2001 couture show, Paris; p106-107: Woven, collection Poetry in Pose AW'11 © Vesna Pesic, photography Nina Sologubenko & Wood, collection Poetry in Pose AW'11 © Vesna Pesic, photography Nina Sologubenko; p111: © *vapour* by KC Lake 2010 (image courtesy of www. kclakemillinery.com); p118: Ivory Ostrich feather headband © Judy Bentinck, photographed by Charlotte Kibbles, www.charlottekibbles.com; p119:© *bone daddy* by KC Lake 2010 (image courtesy of www.kclakemillinery.com); p122-123: © Courtesy of Ascot, photography: Finley Mackay; p124: Antique lace bird cage with diamonds and rubies birds © Philip Treacy for Vogue Gioiello; P126-127: Pinok pok picture hat with bow © Judy Bentinck, photographed by Alistair Cowin, www.alistaircowin.com; p128-129: Athenia headpiece by Louis Mariette © photographed by Philip Volkers; p130: Joy © Gina Foster Millinery; p131: No 5 © Gina Foster Millinery; p132-133: With the Wind, collection Poetry in Pose AW'11, © Vesna Pesic, photography Ashley Low; p134-135: Portrait of Stephen Jones © www.justinephotography.com; p136-137: Circle of Life headpiece by Louis Mariette © photographed by Philip Volkers; pp140, 141, 146-147: © copyright 2011, Vivien Sheriff. Vivien Sheriff * All rights reserved. P142-143: Elizabeth Parker © Dave Wilkinson; p144-145: Diamond eyes moon © Philip Treacy 2001 couture show, Paris; p149: Mote headpiece by Louis Mariette © photographed by Philip Volkers; p150-151: Capunk by Emilie Zanon © Cramcroche; pp158-159, 170: © Popperfoto/Getty Images; p171: Vincent van Gogh; p178-179: Édouard Manet; p180: Henri de Toulouse-Lautrec © Zenodot Verlagsgesellschaft mbH, used under the GNU Free Documentation License; p181: Henri de Toulouse-Lautrec; p182-183: Julia Margaret Cameron; p184: Claude Monet; p185: Paul Cézanne; p187: © Nathalie Novi, *Because Everything Can Change*, 2004, courtesy Josette Gerlier; p189: Spirit of Africa hat by Louis Mariette © photographed by Fabrice Lachant; p190: Hawk hat with feathers cascade and jewel details © Philip Treacy 2001 couture show, Paris.

We gratefully acknowledge the permission granted to use these images. Every possible attempt has been made to identify and contact copyright holders. Any errors or omissions are inadvertent and will be corrected in subsequent editions.

Bibliography

Arwas, V., 2010: *La Vie Parisienne*, 1st ed. London: Papadakis.

Boucher, F., 1967. *A History of Costume in the West*. 1st ed. London: Thames & Hudson.

Broby-Johansen, R., 1968. *Body and Clothes: An Illustrated History of Costume*. 1st ed. London: Faber & Faber Ltd.

Cullen, O., 2009. *Hats: An Anthology by Stephen Jones*. 1st ed. London: V&A Publishing.

Day, J.A.C., 1975. *Decorative Silhouettes of the Twenties*. 1st ed. New York: Dover Publications, Inc.

de la Haye, A. (ed.), 1996. *The Cutting Edge. 50 Years of British Fashion 1947-1997*. 1st ed. London: V&A Publications.

Erte Fashions, 1972. 1st ed. London: Academy Editions Ltd. and New York: St. Martin's Press.

Fifty Hats that Changed the World, 2011. Pub. by the Design Museum. London: Conran Octopus Ltd.

Goldstein Crowe, L. 2011. *Isabella Blow. A Life in Fashion*. 1st ed. London: Quartet Books Limited.

Sternberg, J. & Chapelot, P., 1974. *Pin Up*. 1st ed. London: Academy Editions Ltd. And New York: St. Martin's Press.

Sternberg, J. & Chapelot, P., 1971. *Un Siècle de Pin Up*. 1st ed. Paris: Éditions Planète.

Viollet-le-Duc, E., 1872-1875. *Dictionnaire Raisonné du Mobilier Français de l'Époque Carlovingienne a la Renaissance*. Paris: VE A. Morel & CIE, Éditeurs.

www.hatsuk.com   www.hatshistory.org